LIVING WELL
—OR EVEN BETTER—
ON LESS

LIVING WELL
—OR EVEN BETTER—
ON LESS

Ellen Kunes

A Byron Preiss Visual Publications, Inc., Book

A Perigee Book

Perigee Books
are published by
The Putnam Publishing Group
200 Madison Avenue
New York, NY 10016

Library of Congress Cataloging-in-Publication Data

Kunes, Ellen.
Living well (or even better) on less / by Ellen Kunes.
p. cm.
ISBN 0-399-51693-X (trade pbk.)
1. Finance, Personal. 2. Saving and thrift. I. Title.
HG179.K86   1991   91-8855 CIP
3325.024′01—dc20

Cover design © 1991 by Judith Kazdym Leeds

Printed in the United States of America
1   2   3   4   5   6   7   8   9   10

For my father,
a man who really understands the
value of a dollar

Acknowledgments

My thanks to Maureen Freeburg and Wendy Bagwell for their assistance in researching this book. Also, thanks to Rosemary Ellis for her savvy tips, Babs Lefrak at Byron Preiss Visual Publications, Gene Brissie, and David Freeman for everything else.

Contents

Introduction

Let's face it: In the eighties, we had a lot more money; and in the spirit of the times, we had a great time spending it. Nice homes, fancy cars, exotic vacations, gourmet ice cream—you name it, we bought it.

Not so the nineties. It's quickly becoming clear that we've entered a more frugal era, a time when most of us have far less cash to spend on life's little—and large—luxuries. Trouble is, we've become accustomed to a cushier lifestyle—and living well is a very hard habit to break.

But now you won't have to. In these pages, you will discover hundreds of incredibly easy, never-demeaning ways to save money. In fact, by trying these tips, you'll save thousands of dollars over the course of a year—money that you can use for lavish vacations, your children's college tuitions, a new car, or a down payment on a new (or second) home. What's more, by employing just a few of these ideas, I guarantee that your life will *feel* more luxurious than ever.

1
EATING FOR LESS

Buy the big size. Get the large size in everything; it's almost always cheaper. Best foods to buy in large sizes:

- flour
- sugar
- rice
- condiments
- butter

Freeze the perishables you buy, like butter. Buying the big size also cuts down on trips to the supermarket—a big gas saver.

Dine in. From a culinary standpoint, cocooning is extremely cost-effective. To make it more palatable, invest in one or two terrific cookbooks. And when you've tired of your tried-and-true recipes, swap favorites with your friends.

Avoid buying snack food. You already know that it's fattening; and these foods are also the most expensive at the supermarket. Indeed, they may add as much as 10 percent to your weekly food bill.

Shop the lower shelves at the supermarket. The reason? Store clerks often neglect to reprice items when they're down on the bottom shelves, which means better prices for smart shoppers. Also, be sure to check your receipt before you drive away. You'd be surprised at how many mistakes cashiers make when they're in a hurry.

Go vegetarian at least twice a week. Meat—especially beef, veal and lamb—can put a big dent in your food budget. These days, it's both cheaper and healthier to go meatless from time to time, so invest in a gourmet vegetarian cookbook, like *The Savory Way* by Deborah Madison (Bantam); *The New Laurel's Kitchen* by Laurel Robertson, Carol

Flinders and Brian Ruppenthal (Ten Speed Press); or *Sundays at Moosewood Restaurant* by the Moosewood Collective (Simon and Schuster).

Cook food ahead—in quantity. To avoid those times when you buy expensive order-in or take-out because you haven't the energy to cook, prepare lots of food ahead and freeze it. Lasagna, chili and soup are all great meals to make in quantity on the weekend. Then, divide what you've cooked into one-meal portions for low-cost eating over the course of your work week.

Bring your lunch to work. It's no longer only geeks who bring their lunch to work. Instead of spending $5 on a deli sandwich, make one at home. Buy cold cuts that come in resealable containers to keep ingredients fresh. Bring snacks (yogurt, chips, apples, etc.) from home, too, to cut down on coffee-break costs. Potential savings: $8 a day.

Make your own coffee at work. It doesn't seem all that expensive to buy a cup from a deli or the office coffee cart every day, but the money spent over the course of a year really adds up. ($1 a day = about $260 and more a year!) Instead, invest in

15

an inexpensive coffee maker ($15), buy your favorite brand of coffee and make your own. You'll save at least $200 a year. (Bring a breakfast muffin from home and you'll save even more!)

Keep coffee fresher longer. Leaving a canister of coffee on top of a kitchen cabinet allows it to grow stale more quickly. To keep coffee fresher longer (and get the best taste for the least money), buy your beans whole, keep them in your freezer and then grind them yourself before brewing. (Grinders cost about $10.)

Invest in seal-tight storage containers. Too often, really good food spoils because we throw it into the refrigerator without packing it properly. Tupperware and other vacuum-packed containers really do keep food fresher longer. Some other tips:

- Get freezer wrap for meats and other foods you aren't going to eat immediately.
- Don't let bread and cake get old and moldy if you're going away for a few days. Wrap them in aluminum foil or freezer wrap and store in the freezer.
- Keep bread in the refrigerator in warm weather. It will stay fresher longer.

· Peanut butter is also better off stored in the fridge.

Grow your own food. Just a small part of your backyard can serve as a food-producing fruit/ vegetable garden. What you grow depends on what area of the country you live in, but easy-to-grow crops include tomatoes, corn, strawberries and watermelons. Grow herbs, such as basil, dill and rosemary, indoors on your windowsill for a fresh, inexpensive way to make homemade dishes taste great. To get started, send for a great gardening catalog (free): Jackson & Perkins Co., 2518 South Pacific Highway, Medford, OR 97501. Or phone: (800) 292-GROW or (503) 776-2000.

Join a food co-op. Here's how they work: In exchange for a few hours of work at the co-op each month, you get to buy all sorts of foods—fruits, vegetables, bread, meat, you name it—at wholesale prices. The reason it's cheaper is that the co-op can buy food in bulk, at lower prices.

Shop at "bakery return" thrift stores. These places stock baked goods that went unsold in supermarkets. You'd think that this stuff would be old and moldy, but much of what you can buy in

17

here is just fine: cookies, cakes, cupcakes, brownies—and it's all at least half-price. Big bakers, like Wonder and Entenmann's, run these stores, so check your local yellow pages.

Make food look more appetizing. By setting a beautiful table and using your good dishes, you won't miss dining out as much. Use cloth napkins and serve dinners restaurant-style, delivering carefully arranged food to each diner. Bonus: Everyone will probably eat less because meals have been portioned out in advance—good for the pocketbook *and* the scale.

Throw potluck dinners. Ask each guest to bring a course. It's much less expensive than giving a dinner party all by yourself—and everybody gets a chance to show off his or her best recipes.

Don't buy bottled water. Stick with tap water, unless yours tastes terrible or is known to be unhealthy. The bottled stuff is very expensive and new studies show that it may contain as many pollutants—or more—than what comes out of your faucet.

Go to great restaurants—for lunch. You can eat the same swell cooking and get that "hot" restaurant ambience for far less than you'd pay at dinnertime. (Many good restaurants have basically the same menu at lunchtime, only the prices are lower.) Do this while on vacation, too. Visit the most elegant eateries in Paris at midday for better service and prices.

Have a "happy hour" dinner. Many restaurants have happy hours, usually from 5 P.M. to 7 P.M., when, for the price of a single drink, you can choose from an array of tasty appetizers like chicken wings, mini-pizzas, crab cakes and more.

Look for early-bird or pre-theater specials. Restaurants across the country offer the same menu and meals at a deep discount—as long as you get there before a certain time, usually 7 P.M. Call your favorite eateries to see if they offer such specials.

Clip those "two-for-one" dining coupons. Many restaurants (particularly just-opened eateries) offer two dinners for the price of one. Take advantage of such deals, and also those that offer $5 or more off the cost of your meal.

Order appetizers, not entrées. Many restaurants serve up large appetizer portions, which cost half the price of an entrée. Instead of ordering an appetizer and an entrée, get two appetizers and fill up for less.

Learn a few basics about ordering wine.

- Avoid expensive French and California wines.
- Try Chilean and Spanish wines; they're usually quite good for far less cash.
- When in season (normally from the end of November to May), order Beaujolais Nouveau ("new" French Beaujolais), which tastes great and normally costs less than $10 a bottle.
- When buying wine for a cocktail party, try these other low-priced favorites: 1985 Poppy Hill Zinfandel ($7); Charles de Fere, Brut, Blanc de Blanc ($8.99); the Monterey Vineyard Classic White ($4.27); 1987 Masson Chardonnay ($7.32).

Ask prices for off-menu specials. Everyone feels slightly embarrassed about asking the cost of those fabulous-sounding specials that are recited by the waiter (usually without mention of price). Restaurants count on such shyness and charge extra-high prices for specials. So ask the prices and then avoid those dishes if the cost seems exorbitant.

When ordering, ask if the restaurant serves "family style." Instead of having everyone at the table order his/her own expensive entrée, have big plates of just two or three dishes served up. And share desserts; people rarely finish theirs, and you'll help keep each other slim.

Always ask for a doggie bag. These days, even the finest restaurants will do up a doggie bag for you. This can save you at least one future meal, and if you don't want to eat last night's leftovers the very next day, freeze them.

Ask restaurants for their recipes. Often, chefs are flattered and happy to tell you how they prepared a favorite dish. Then, do it at home—and save.

Don't pay for the whole table with your credit card. Don't have everyone else hand you cash, and then pay your share and the rest of the bill with your card. You may end up using that cash in the next few days and then be left with a hefty bill at the end of the month. If you have to use your card, collect everyone's cash and store it in an envelope. The best idea is to put it right into your checking account.

Go to "all-you-can-eat" brunch buffets. This is a great way to fill your family up for a low price—and get a dining-out experience.

Get fast-food savvy. Order the package meal—you know, the hamburger, fries and cola sold for one price—rather than à la carte at your favorite fast-food eatery. You may prefer to get just the burger and cola (fries are so fattening!), but the cost of the package is often lower than just those two items. (Give the fries to another diner.)

2
GETTING AROUND FOR LESS

Get the lowest price on a new car. To get the best deal, know what the car dealer actually paid for a car. Don't believe the "invoice cost" quoted in ads; it's often inflated. Instead, call Carputer International for the dealer price of the car you want. Call: (800) 722-4440 ($1 per minute; the first minute is free). Or consult *Edmund's New Car Prices* for prices; then try to bargain dealers down to $300–$500 over that price. The best time to buy a car? Just before Christmas, when business is slow, and in January and February. When *not* to buy: From March to June, when people start gearing up for summer travel, and in the early fall when the hot new models hit the showrooms. Another tip: Keep your eyes open for financing sales offering rebates or reductions on interest rates.

Rent the same model car you plan to buy. Before investing in a new car, take a similar model for a long, unpressured spin by renting it for a weekend. You can even rent it from your auto dealer. Even Cadillac recently had free weekend tryouts for its cars, so ask the dealer before you decide to buy.

Find less expensive auto insurance. By buying a car model with a lower rate of theft (and one that is less easily damaged), you can save hundreds of dollars each year. Insurance companies often offer discounts to owners of such autos. These include luxury cars (like the Chrysler Fifth Avenue), family cars (like the Mercury Sable and Buick LeSabre), mini-vans (like the Dodge Caravan) and imports (like the Toyota Camry and Tercel). For word on where to find the cheapest auto insurance, subscribe to the auto newsletter *Nutz & Boltz* ($30 a year), Box 123, Butler, MD 21023-0123. It offers *lots* of useful information on cars and the auto industry.

Get higher deductible on car collision insurance. You can cut your auto insurance fees by 25 percent by increasing your deductible from $100 to $500. Also, if you already have personal medical and hospitalization coverage, you don't need this coverage in your auto insurance. And don't pick up insurance "frills" such as towing costs. It's cheaper to get your own service (the American Automobile Association, AAA, offers membership for $20–$30 per year and offers free towing, road service and trip planning).

Drop collision insurance if you're driving an older model. When the price of collision insurance is more than a tenth of the value of the old car, according to the latest National Automobile Dealers Association's Official Used Car Guide, it's not worth the extra expense (which can add up to thousands of dollars over the life of the car). The NADA Official Used Car Guide, by the way, includes lots of useful information and can be ordered for $43 by calling (800) 544-6232.

More car insurance discounts. You can get an even deeper discount for having such add-ons as air bags, automatic seat belts and antitheft devices. Ask your insurance company about the insurance-lowering incentives it offers.

Get savvy about car repairs. There are a variety of ways to keep car repair costs down and insure that you won't get ripped off. To begin with, it's always wise to know as much as possible about your car. So consider taking a course in auto mechanics. When a car mechanic evaluates your car and points out that new parts are needed, get a written itemized estimate, with the cost of each part noted. Then check the retail price of the parts at the local auto-parts store to see if the prices quoted by the mechanic are in the same ballpark. Have the mechanic save all discarded parts for you to inspect. If you think that you've been overcharged, ask to see the shop's "flat-rate" manual (which gives the factory rate for car parts and the average rate for labor). The one to look at: *Chilton's Motor/Age Labor Guide and Parts Manual,* which can be found at your local library. Finally, always give preference to shops that are willing to warrant their work.

Take public transportation whenever possible. Do this just a few times a week and save substantially on gas and tolls. You'll contribute to an environmental savings at the same time.

Walk instead of taking taxis. Cabs are incredibly expensive, and in bad-traffic cities like New York,

San Francisco, Chicago and Washington, D.C., it's sometimes faster to get where you're going via the sidewalks instead of the backseat of a cab, watching the meter tick away while stuck in a gridlock.

Buy your bridge and tunnel tokens or mass-transit tickets in bulk. Many state transit authorities offer discounts for tokens or tickets bought in large quantities. Some also offer discounted monthly passes. And if you're a senior citizen, know that many transit systems offer you discounted passes.

Pump your own gas. You can save as much as 5 cents a gallon on self-service gasoline. Pay in cash instead of credit card and save another 4 cents a gallon.

Get a fuel-efficient car. According to the Environmental Protection Agency, the ten most fuel-efficient cars are (listed by miles per gallon, city driving):

- Geo Metro-XFI (53)
- Honda CRX HF (49)
- Geo Metro-LSI (45)
- Suzuki Swift (45)

- Daihatsu Charade (38)
- Volkswagen Jetta (37)
- Ford Festiva (35)
- Subaru Justy (33)
- Toyota Tercel (33)
- Mitsubishi Eclipse (31)

Drive slower and save. When you drive at 55 miles per hour, you use about one-third less fuel in some models than you would driving the same distance at 70 miles per hour.

On road trips, leave early in the morning to avoid rush-hour traffic jams. They're big gas-wasters.

Plan your driving routes ahead to avoid congested streets.

Keep baggage light. Having lots of weight in the trunk burns extra gas, as does heavy or bulky rooftop cargo (aerodynamics really do affect a car's performance).

Buy a car with a light-colored exterior and interior. The reason? Dark colors absorb heat, increasing the need for costly air-conditioning.

Use regular unleaded gas. More than 90 percent of cars don't require premium gasoline, which costs on average 15 cents more per gallon than regular gas. Also, for better gas mileage, keep your car in tune.

Start carpooling. To save on the cost of commuting, group up. Everyone in the car shares the expenses for gas, tolls and parking. Most of the week, you'll have some extra sleep and/or newspaper-reading time, too. Many areas have express lanes for car pools, so you can probably leave home later, too. There's another big bonus: Auto insurance companies offer as much as a 20 percent discount on premiums to carpoolers because participants drive less than solo commuters.

Garage your car. You won't have to wash it as often, its life span will increase and it's less likely to be broken into or hit by other cars, all resulting in lower insurance premiums and higher resale value.

3

MONEY
FOR LESS

Pay off your credit cards in full every month.
That way, you avoid the charges of up to 20 percent—and starting this year, none of that money is tax-deductible. If you can't pay it in full, put the card away so you won't add to the debt, and pay as much as you can in monthly increments.

Put aside money in your savings account with every paycheck. Many companies will automatically transfer a preset amount from your paycheck into a savings account. Having just $25 taken from your check each week will get you more than $1,200 by the end of a year.

Keep a bowl near the front door for loose change. It really does add up. When the bowl is full, get paper rolls from the bank, roll up the change and get some dollar bills back. You'll be surprised how much has accumulated in pennies, nickels and dimes (quarters are for laundry).

Give out allowances in small bills. This way your child won't spend it all at once. If your child's allowance is $5 a week, give him/her five one-dollar bills. Then suggest he/she take at least one of those bills and put it in a piggy bank.

Take out a personal or home-equity loan. If you owe $2,000 or more on your credit cards, pay the cards off at once with a loan. Reason? These types of loans have a much lower rate of interest (about 10–12 percent) than that charged by credit-card companies (up to 19 percent). Also, the interest on home-equity and personal loans may be 100 percent tax-deductible.

Get low-interest credit cards. Some banks offer extra-low rates (like 12–14 percent) for their cards. To find out where to apply, send for "Fair Deal List," which lists more than fifty banks around the country that offer low-interest-rate charge cards. Send $1.50 to BankCard Holders of America, 560 Herndon Parkway, Suite 120, Herndon, VA 22070. Also, look for cards with a low annual fee or no fee, and which have a long "grace" period: 25–30 days between the first billing and the day interest starts accruing.

Join a credit-card registry. It isn't a bad idea if you have a stack of credit cards in your wallet and are an easy mark for pickpockets. It only costs between $12 and $15 for peace of mind. But if you have only a couple of cards, don't bother. Likewise, check to see if you're already covered for credit-card theft in your homeowner's or renter's insurance policy. If so, you don't need this coverage. And whatever you do, don't give your credit-card numbers out over the phone to someone claiming to be from a card "protection" agency—it could be a scam.

Pay cash whenever possible. For one thing, you'll probably spend less if you limit your purchases to what you have in your pockets. And another good reason to pay in cash: Many stores will give a discount if you use cash because they won't have to pay a credit-card fee.

Limit trips to the cash machine to once a week.
Figure out how much you'll need and stick to that
amount. You'll have to do some budgeting, but
you'll find you've saved a lot at the end of the
month. Leave your cash card at home the rest of
the time to keep from making unnecessary with-
drawals.

Round down your bank machine withdrawal.
Often, cash machines will give out only certain
denominations (usually tens and twenties). If the
machine has run out of the smaller denomina-
tion, take out that much less instead of more (e.g.,
if you want $150 and the machine is giving out
only twenties, take out $140, not $160).

Get savvy about medical insurance. You can
lower the annual premium by increasing your
insurance deductible. Also, always alert doctors
to how much of their bills you, not the insurance
company, must pay. They may quote a lower
price for their services. Finally, always check
bills for errors: Doctors make mistakes about
money, just like you.

Refinance your mortgage. Because the recession
has caused interest rates to go down, it's wise to

try to get a lower mortgage. How to tell if you'll benefit: If the difference between your current mortgage and the new, lower rate is at least 2 percentage points, and if you plan to stay in the same home for at least another 3 years, you could save thousands of dollars over the life of the loan. One important tip: Try to refinance through your current lender in order to save money on closing costs, title search and points.

Buy stock through a discount broker. These brokers can save you up to 90 percent on commission costs—as long as you do your own research on the stocks. The names of the big three: Quick & Reilly, Inc., Fidelity Brokerage Services, Inc., and Charles Schwab & Co.

Consolidate your savings, checking and other accounts in one bank. The reason? Many banks now have minimum-balance requirements for free checking, cash-machine use and other services. Putting accounts together makes it easier to meet that minimum balance. The savings per month: $20 or more. One word of warning: You're only insured for up to $100,000 per person, so don't keep more than that in one bank.

Get life insurance from discount brokers. Now there are brokers who can sell life insurance policies at a 20–30 percent discount. For names of discount brokers in your area, call the Council of Life Insurance Consultants at (800) 533-0777.

Don't get taken by fakes. Send away for "Investment Swindles: How They Work and How to Avoid Them." This free pamphlet describes tactics swindlers employ, and teaches potential victims how to smell a rat. Write: Consumer Information Center, Item 548X, Pueblo, CO 81009.

Tax smarts for free. Send for the 1991 Tax Planning Guide, which provides information on deducting expenses, retirement planning and more. Write to: Weber, Lipshie & Co., Marketing Department, 1430 Broadway, New York, NY 10018. It's free.

Get a big tax break. Set up an account for each child under age 14, with each account earning assets up to $1,000 each year. The point: The first $500 of investment income earned by kids under 14 is totally tax-free. The next $500 is taxed at 15 percent—far below the parents' rate (up to 33 percent). Keep in mind that once the kids' earnings exceed $1,000, their money is taxed at *your* rate.

Conduct a scholarship search. Even if your kids aren't eligible for financial aid, you can still get money for their education. The College Financial Planning Service lists more than $10 billion in private-sector scholarships in its computer data bank. The cost of a search is $45. This fee, by the way, is refundable if within two weeks it doesn't provide you with the name of a scholarship worth at least $100 for which your child qualifies. Call: (800) 346-6401.

Scope out great—but inexpensive—colleges. There are a number of state schools that are almost as prestigious as the Ivy League, but they charge much less in tuition and other fees. These include:

- The University of California, Berkeley (tuition is $1,640 yearly for state residents; $7,556 for nonresidents)
- The University of Georgia, Athens ($2,001 for state residents; $5,313 for nonresidents)
- The University of Illinois, Urbana–Champaign ($2,778 for residents; $6,328 for nonresidents)

- The University of New Hampshire, Durham ($3,558 for residents; $9,638 for nonresidents)
- The University of North Carolina, Chapel Hill ($1,018 for residents; $5,520 for nonresidents)

Continuing education is tax-deductible. If it's required by your employer, you can write it off. However, if you take classes to learn a new job, the expenses are not deductible.

4

FUN
FOR LESS

Borrow books from the library. Instead of buying them, check your reads out at the local library. At many, you can put dibs on the latest best-seller, and the library will call you when it comes in. Save $5–$10 a week.

Sell books you don't need. For books you've already bought but no longer need—don't throw or give them away. You can get as much as half the original cost by taking used books to a second-hand bookstore.

Learn to trust a movie critic. There's probably one particular film reviewer who often likes or dislikes the same movies that you do. Before slapping down $7 for a flick, check to see what your favorite critic said. If he/she didn't give it a rave, wait for it to come out on video.

Go to early-bird movies. When possible, see a first-run film before dinner and save up to $8 for a pair of tickets.

Try to rent from video stores at off-peak (often midweek) rates. Save up to $3 a flick. Many also offer two-for-one deals. Others that ordinarily allow you to keep the movie for two days give bonuses for early returns. You can also rent videos from the library. In many public libraries, movie videos can be checked out along with the books.

When throwing a party, buy beer from a distributor. When you need several cases, the distributor's price will be much lower than that of a supermarket or liquor store. Other ways to save when throwing a bash: Instead of having a series of medium-size fetes over the course of the year, have one big party for your friends. Instead of hiring a bartender, have your spouse or a friend play the role for the first drink and then suggest that people mix their own. Also, serve wine and punches instead of mixed drinks to cut down on the cost of liquor. Get inexpensive mixers—orange juice, soda, etc.—you don't need to buy name brands. Remember that for mixed drinks, the lower-price vodka is just fine (but don't skimp on gin or scotch).

Buy a few games to play at home. And then invite friends over for an informal party. Trivial Pursuit, charades or Pictionary will keep you all entertained, for free. (Saves on baby-sitting, too.)

Get your theater tickets at half-price. In many cities, you can get great seats for top shows and concerts at half-price booths. You'd be surprised how easy it is to get good seats, especially for a play that's been running for a while. The only drawback is that the performances are usually on the same day.

Buy standing-room theater tickets: Especially when it's an incredibly popular musical—or when a big star is in the cast—theaters offer standing-room tickets for a fraction (perhaps $10!) of the full-price seats. The standing room is usually behind the last row of the orehestra, so the view is often better than that in the mezza-nine. What's more, if you see that certain seats in front of you are still unoccupied by the end of the first act, the ushers will often let you sit for the second act.

Take advantage of senior-citizen discounts. Seniors get all sorts of great discounts on theater, ballet, movie and sports tickets, and for tennis clubs, department stores, public transportation, etc. If you qualify, take advantage of all the dis-counts offered.

Drop those cable movie channels. They're costly, and you don't get to choose the films you'd like to see as you can when renting videos. They show the same movies a zillion times each month, and you can rent several videos for the monthly fee.

Swap magazines with your friends. Cut back on your subscription list, limiting yourself to your three or four favorite magazines. Once you've finished reading them, trade them with pals who subscribe to different ones. Also, when you renew your subscriptions, renew for the longest term for maximum savings.

Take advantage of all free-subscription offers.
Next time you get a free one-month (or longer)
subscription to a magazine, or an offer for a free
book, go ahead and try it. Just be sure that you
won't be obligated to buy anything (read the fine
print carefully). When you receive a bill for a
year's worth of periodicals, simply write "cancel"
on the card (unless you love the magazine enough
to want to get a subscription). By the way, it's
wise to get magazine subscriptions through special "subscription services," which often offer far
lower rates than those offered by the magazine
itself. One good one is University Subscription
Service, which offers lower rates to students and
teachers of all ages. Write: 1213 Butterfield Road,
Downer's Grove, IL 60515-9968 for more information.

Buy your CDs secondhand. Many music stores
are selling used CDs that are a third to a half the
price of new, and they sound just as wonderful.
What's more, many types of music sound just fine
on cassettes—also about half the price of CDs—so
save by buying cassettes when you can.

Trade cassettes with friends. Instead of buying
every new tape as it comes out, swap tapes with

friends—and cut your cassette-buying costs in half.

Re-record old prerecorded cassettes. When you're sure you won't want to listen to those old tunes, put a piece of Scotch tape over the hole on the top and tape new music borrowed from a friend.

Buy cheaper seats for sporting events. Chances are, you'll be able to move into better seats by the second inning or quarter.

Bring your own food to the ballpark or arena. It will cost a fraction of the lukewarm hot dogs on soggy buns.

Buy a used personal computer. You can buy used machines, in top condition, for up to 80 percent off the list price. To buy, look in the classified section of the newspaper or in a computer magazine under "Used Computers." Always ask for a warranty, costing around 15 percent of the sale price, and before buying, check out the broker's track record with the Better Business Bureau.

Buy computer software by mail. Get up to 50 percent off on all programs from the mail-order computer software firm 800-Software. Call (800) 888-4880 for a free catalog.

Take a country-club deduction. If you use any sort of club for business purposes—like entertaining a client—you can get a tax write-off for about 50 percent of the time you're there.

Go to free concerts and plays. In most cities, all sorts of free music and theater are available—often in beautiful outdoor settings. For more information about free performances, check local newspapers or call your local chamber of commerce.

Swap baby-sitting chores. To cut down on the high cost of baby-sitting, set up a baby-sitters club with a few neighbors and friends. On nights when you're going to be home with the kids anyway, baby-sit one or two other children. Then, when you want a night off, drop your kids with the parents staying at home that night. (This probably won't work on Saturday nights, but you will get more nights out on the town during the week.)

Create your own play group. Instead of paying for very young children to meet each other, organize a play group in your neighborhood. Each mom (or dad) serves as host once every week or so.

Share your baby-sitters. When you're going out with a couple that also has young children, share the same baby-sitter. Offer to pay him/her a higher rate (which can still be lower than what you'd spend for two separate sitters). What's more, you'll only need to make one call to find out if all the children are okay.

Wait for best-sellers to come out in paperback. Hot titles are often issued in softcover editions just a few months after their hardcover debuts.

5

DRESSING FOR LESS

Cut back on dry cleaning. You can hand-wash many items that say "dry-clean only," such as wool sweaters and silk blouses. The only clothes to continue dry-cleaning are those that have a lining, such as tailored jackets or clothes with "interfacing"—which can shrink if hand-washed. It could save you $10 a week.

Use only a little bleach. When laundering your clothes, remember that a little bleach goes a long way. Too much will cause your garments to wear out sooner.

Launder and iron (or get a friend to iron) your shirts. The cost of sending them to the cleaners or Chinese laundry is astronomical, and if you grab them out of the dryer quickly, they only need a little touching up.

Cut buttons off clothes before throwing them away. Many garments are rendered unwearable because you lose a button that you can't match. Snip off whole sets of buttons from old blouses to save a blouse or jacket you love. (FYI: Cary Grant used to do this!)

For routine hemming, go to a dry cleaner instead of a tailor. Many dry cleaners offer simple tailoring services—for less than a regular tailor.

Don't throw away unfashionable but good clothes. Instead, send them out to be refurbished and made fashionable again. Have expensive silk ties made shorter, wider or skinnier by sending them to Movieland Tie Service, 8170 West Third Street, Los Angeles, CA 90048. Their phone number is (213) 653-0866. Cost: from $4–$15 per tie, minimum four ties per mail order. For costly suits and dresses with burn holes or tears, send them to a super reweaver—the one other reweavers send their toughest requests to: Alice Zotta, 2 West 45th Street, Room 1504, New York, NY 10036. Minimum $10 per item. You pay when the item is returned to you.

Resell what you don't need. Never ever just throw out what no longer fits or what you don't like. Head for a secondhand store and sell your stuff there.

Remember the bargain calendar. Just as you can count on the four seasons, you can rely on sales of certain products taking place at the same time every year. Here, a listing of what goes on sale when:

- Dresses: January, April, June, November
- Lingerie: January, May, July
- Shoes: (men's and women's) January, July, November, December; (boys' and girls') January, March, July
- Handbags: January, May, July
- Sportswear: January, February, May, July
- Costume and Fine Jewelry: January

Buy clothes from catalogs. They really are cheaper, and for good reason: Since there's no expensive storefront, there's no big retail markup and the savings are passed on to you. Our favorites include:

- *J. Crew:* Knock-around basics for weekends in fun colors. Best buys are cotton T-shirts, $12; roll-neck sweaters, $48; barn jackets, $98. For a catalog, call (800) 562-0258.
- *Victoria's Secret:* Swell-looking lingerie, along with slinky dresses and bathing suits. Best bets are the sexy bras and bikinis. For a catalog, call (800) 888-8200.
- *Tweeds:* Great weekend clothing with European styling. Best bets are big poet shirts in washed silk, and cotton turtlenecks in 17 colors for $19. For a catalog, call (800) 999-7997.
- *Spiegel:* Features clothes from big-name designers such as Anne Klein, DKNY, Ellen Tracy and Adrienne Vittadini. Great selection and lots of terrific career clothes. For a catalog ($3), call (800) 345-4500.
- *Patagonia:* High-tech sportswear in bright colors for climbing, hiking, skiing—all kinds of heavy-duty outdoor activity. For a catalog (printed on recycled paper), call (800) 638-6464.

• *The J. Peterman Company:* Great authentic, eclectic sportswear. Novelty items like real English riding boots, mackintosh raincoats, etc. For a catalog, call (800) 231-7341.

Shop for designer clothes at factory outlets. These days, whole towns have become factory outlet centers, places where you can find designer clothes for 40–70 percent off retail—and even more. (In addition to apparel, outlets sell all sorts of household goods, luggage, electronics, sporting goods—the list goes on.) The kinds of items you'll find here are factory irregulars, samples and discontinued items. According to *Outletbound,* a yearly guide to the nation's outlet stores (send $5.95 to Box 1255, Orange, CT 06477), the top ten outlet towns are: Freeport, Maine; Kittery, Maine; Woodbury Common in Central Valley, New York; Reading, Pennsylvania; Boaz, Alabama; Pigeon Forge, Tennessee; Orlando, Florida; City of Commerce, California; Birch Run, Michigan; Kenosha, Wisconsin.

Have clothes made for you. It sounds like the height of luxury, but having a seamstress sew clothes for you can actually save you money. Here's what to do: Get pictures of a style you love—of all sides of the garment, if possible. See if the style is included in a pattern book (available at sewing stores). Take the photo or pattern to a seamstress/tailor recommended to you. (It's wise to try the person out on an easy job, such as altering a pair of pants or a skirt.) You may also be asked to find the material you want. It's possible to save $100 on a dress or suit—and chances are, your outfit will be more finely made than the store-bought version.

Learn how to work a clothing sale. Knowing how to buy swell stuff while others are grabbing around you is truly an art. To begin with, always get to sales early. Those who get the best deals are standing in line at 6 A.M., and later they've got the great buys in hand. Plan ahead what you really need, and try not to get waylaid in a different department, or you could come away without the clothes you were really looking for. For women, wear tight-fitting clothes, like leggings and a tank top. That way, if the dressing rooms are absolutely packed, you can try things on in a corner without embarrassment. Also, in the excitement of a sale, don't get carried away. Don't buy clothes that don't fit perfectly or you'll be wasting money rather than saving it. Shopping in pairs is also wise. You need a friend for a fast second opinion, since you probably won't be allowed to put any items on hold, and you may not completely trust the salesperson's opinion. Finally, if you spy any imperfections that haven't been accounted for in the sale price—marked "as is"—ask a store clerk if the item can be marked down even more.

Buy designer duds at swell secondhand shops. These days, there are terrific secondhand, "gently-worn" designer clothing stores, where you can get the kind of couture that Jackie O. dons—for a song. (If you live in New York or LA, there's a good chance that a celebrity traded in those one-of-a-kind silks and satins.) Clothes that retailed for $1,000 and up can be had at these shops for a few hundred—or less. Check your yellow pages.

Get a personal shopper. Having someone else shop *for* you sounds like the luxury of luxuries, but this service, now offered by most large department stores, is almost always free and a great money and time saver. The reason? Personal shoppers know your taste, your size and the size of your wallet. When something that you need or love goes on sale, they'll hold the item for you, before other shoppers get a crack at it. Personal shoppers will also keep an eye open for sales on children's clothing. Chances are, you'll make fewer costly "mistakes" when choosing clothes with a shopper, and using the service often means you get free alterations, too. What's more, the dressing room areas open to those using the service are often more luxurious than regular fitting rooms, and you may be offered free coffee, mineral water—or even lunch—for trying a department store's shopping service. By the way, don't fear that you have to be prepared to spend a minimum of a few hundred dollars. Almost all stores offer this service with no minimum purchase required.

Go to sample sales. These are sales of top-of-the-line designer clothes, often held at the designer's offices or showrooms, for up to 90 percent off the retail prices. Sometimes, "demonstration" models of designs featured in the fashion magazines can be found here; what's more, these clothes are the very ones you'll see in department stores that season. Sample sales take place mostly in New York and Los Angeles—the big clothing centers—but now they're cropping up in other cities. To find out where and when sales are held in New York, call the Bargain Hotline ($1.95 the first minute; 75 cents every minute thereafter). Call: (212) 540-0123 for weekly updates on sales.

Rent formal wear for fancy events. Forget about investing $500 or more in a dress you'll never be able to wear again. There are shops across the country that rent fabulous designer dresses—ones you could never afford to buy—for one-time use. You can even rent a wedding dress that retails for $5,000 (you pay $200)! Look in your yellow pages.

Throw a swap meet for kids' clothes. Face it: Children's clothing is becoming terribly expensive, and kids tend to outgrow those great-looking styles before they've had time to put holes in them. That is why it's smart to organize a swap session with your friends. With everyone laying out their kids' barely broken-in duds, you're sure to find great clothes for your children—without spending a dime.

Buy solid colors. Prints go out of style much more quickly. Get fabrics that can be worn year-round, like lightweight wool gabardines, cotton knits and jerseys.

Buy opaque panty hose. They last much longer than sheerer stuff. And make sure the toes are reinforced to avoid runs. Hand-wash hosiery in mild facial soap to extend their lives even longer.

Keep shoes in good repair. It costs a lot less to resole or reheel a pair of shoes than to replace them.

6
LOOKING GOOD FOR LESS

Get a home manicure kit. With a little practice, you can save on costly salon manicures and pedicures. Save $8 a week.

Rent exercise videos. Instead of rejoining that expensive health club that you rarely visit anyway, get a good workout from Jane Fonda and others for only a few dollars a session. If you find yourself working out often, it even pays to buy the tape.

Buy inexpensive home exercise equipment. Wait until the local sporting goods emporium is having a clearance sale, or send for a free catalog from Better Health, which sells brand-name stationary bikes, treadmills, rowing machines, free weights and more for up to 50 percent off. Call for a catalog: (718) 436-4693.

Join an inexpensive health club. If you can't motivate yourself to work out at home, tour a number of athletic clubs in your area. Try to sign up on a month-by-month basis so you don't get locked into a club membership that you don't really use. Charge the initial fees on a credit card, so if there's any dispute, the credit-card company can cancel payment. Also, don't sign a contract without reading it very carefully. Many health facilities are run by sleazy operators who will tell you about money-back guarantees but will then ask you to sign a contract that makes no such promises. The least expensive clubs around are usually Y's. If there isn't a good one in your area, call the IRSA (the International Racquet Sports Association 800-232-4772) for suggestions for reputable inexpensive clubs in your area. And before you fork over any money, call the Better Business Bureau to see if complaints have been lodged against the club you're thinking of joining.

Book court time at off-hours. You'd be surprised at how much you can save (sometimes 50 percent!) by reserving tennis or racquetball courts early in the A.M. or later in the evening (after 10 P.M.). Of course, it takes a little more effort to get to your workout at these hours, but in some ways it's much more fun. There are fewer people around to get in the way of your game. Another idea: Join a round-robin tournament; the court time is usually free, plus you get plenty of calorie-burning competition.

Buy your workouts—in quantity. It's usually less expensive to buy your exercise classes in bulk. For example, get ten aerobics classes for the price of eight, and so on. But, before paying for all those aerobics classes up front, always ask to take a trial class first to make sure you'll really want to come back for more.

Join a community swimming pool instead of building your own. It sounds like the ultimate dream to have a pool in your own backyard, but the upkeep is terribly expensive, and unless you can keep your eye on it at all hours, it's probably not safe for your kids. They'll probably have more fun at a pool club, where events and lessons are often organized and offered free, and they'll be much safer because lifeguards are always on duty.

Buy generic aspirin, acetaminophen or ibu-profen. The formulas are the same as for the name brands, but the costs are a fraction. Look for similar savings on other over-the-counter drugs, like cold and allergy relievers.

Throw a makeup swap party. Everyone makes cosmetic-buying mistakes. To unload bad buys—and pick up better choices free of charge—invite friends to a swap party. How it works: Everyone throws their "giveaways" on a table—and then starts grabbing.

Take advantage of free make-overs. When it comes to cosmetics, it's always wise to try prod-ucts on *before* you buy. Allow the cosmetician to demonstrate makeup and, whenever possible, get samples first and use the product for a few days before actually making a purchase.

Always get a gift with cosmetic purchases. We all love getting those terrific little bags filled with sample sizes of products when we spend, say, $10 or more on a certain brand of makeup. Don't ever buy a cosmetic simply to get the gift, but do take advantage of special offers—and always ask if special gifts are available—some stores don't always tell customers.

Buy generic-brand cosmetics. They're made of the same stuff as those ultra-expensive brand names, but they can cost up to 70 percent less.

Buy name-brand cosmetics by mail. Beauty Boutique sells cosmetics by Giorgio, Elizabeth Arden, Max Factor, Estee Lauder and Revlon for up to 90 percent off. Call for a free catalog: (216) 826-3008.

Use stick or roll-on antiperspirant/deodorant. It lasts much longer than aerosol.

Stay away from pump toothpastes. Again, these don't last as long as regular tubes do. Also, you need less toothpaste than you think.

Buy combination shampoo/conditioners. For the same price as shampoo alone, these combos leave your hair soft and manageable—and they cut down on your time in the shower. To make shampoo or conditioner last twice as long, cut it with tap water when the bottle's half-empty.

Take showers instead of baths. This can save up to half the cost of heating hot water. Another idea: Put a flow-control valve in your showerhead to save even more.

Keep your soap out of the spray in the shower. It lasts a lot longer when it isn't being constantly bombarded with water.

Get a designer haircut—for free. Many top-of-the-line salons give free haircuts from staff trainees. Call a designer salon in your city for more information. Also, salons often offer package deals that combine a wash, cut, perm or coloring for far less than their separate costs.

Pamper yourself by buying a pretty soap or bath oil every week. These are incredibly inexpensive little luxuries which can make you feel better about cutting back costs in other areas of your life. You may not be able to afford a new house or car, but you can make your body look and smell great—for pennies.

7

HOME
FOR LESS

Get a thermostat timer. It will automatically lower the temperature when you're not in the house or when you're asleep. (By the way, for each degree the thermostat is turned down, you'll reduce your fuel bill by 2 percent.) It can also turn on the air conditioner right before you get home so you don't need to leave it running all day during the summer.

Get a free energy audit. Call your utility company for one. They should be able to tell you how to save money on electricity and gas, and give information on where you need to caulk and insulate to cut fuel costs. Also, send for the free

"Tips on Ways to Save Energy" from the U.S. Department of Energy. Call (800) 523-2929.

Buy fuel oil in summer. That's when prices are lower. Studies show that families in northern states can save more than $250 a year in heating bills this way. Another energy saver: Put an insulation blanket over the hot-water heater—this could save another $40 a year.

Save electricity with better lighting. You'll save on utility bills if you use low-wattage incandescent bulbs and compact fluorescent bulbs. (These last ten times as long as conventional bulbs and use one-fourth the electricity.) Also, be sure to replace dead or flickering fluorescents promptly; even burned-out lamps draw power if they're turned on. Installing a dimmer switch can also lower your electric bills while it reduces glare in your home.

Use fans instead of your air conditioner. Fans use only 10 percent of the electricity that air conditioners use. Get ceiling paddle fans for the bedrooms (it's usually cooler at night, so the a/c isn't always necessary). Also save on air-conditioning (and heating) costs by closing off the rooms (and vents) in your home that aren't being used.

Get an energy-efficient refrigerator. Refrigerators and freezers are big energy-burners. Cut your bill by hundreds by getting a fridge/freezer that operates on less than 500 kilowatt hours annually. If you can't afford a new fridge now, turn the temperature up to 40°F (and the freezer to 5°F) to lower electricity costs by about 25 percent.

Cut fuel costs even more by sending away for "Oil and Gas Heating Systems Maintenance and Improvement." It offers ways to save money by upgrading or even replacing your heating system. Write: Educational Resources Office, Massachusetts Audubon Society, Lincoln, MA 01773. ($3)

Run the dishwasher instead of hand-washing your dishes. You'll use much less hot water that way. Be sure it's full before starting for peak efficiency.

Cut your phone bill. By using the phone book to find numbers, you'll save; each call to directory assistance can cost up to 30 cents. Also, have several long-distance companies audit your monthly bills. Then choose the company that gives the least expensive audit. For a good comparison of the different companies and the rates they offer, get "Tele-Tips Residential Long Distance Comparison Chart." Send $1 and a self-addressed, stamped envelope to TRAC, P.O. Box 12038, Washington, DC 20005.

Choose a long-distance service that offers great incentives. For instance, those who use MCI get frequent-flyer miles on American Airlines. The longer you talk, the more free miles you get.

Stop your kids from making expensive toll calls. By getting a phone-call restricter, which prevents kids from dialing certain 900 numbers and national/local numbers, you can keep your kids from using them. Costs about $90.

Keep your long-distance calls short. Write down what you need to talk about before you make the call. And take note of when calling rates are lowest—like on weekends—and save your longest calls for then.

Own your phone—don't rent. These days, renting a basic touch-tone phone costs about $61 a year—about $10 more than the cost of buying the same model.

Don't pay for an unlisted phone number. It can cost $100 a year. Instead, have your number listed in the phone directory under a fictitious name (but the correct address) and only give out that name and number to close friends and relatives.

When making credit-card calls, dial yourself. Some long-distance companies charge an additional 75 cents when the operator enters the card number for you. If the operator comes on the line before you begin direct dialing, mention that you're trying to dial yourself and ask for the direct-dial rate.

Make your own cleaning fluids. To save money *and* keep the environment clean, make your own all-purpose cleaner by mixing 1 teaspoon vegetable-based liquid soap (like Dr. Bronner's) or 1 teaspoon of borax into a quart of warm water. Add a squeeze of lemon to cut grease and grime. For drain cleaner: Take a handful of baking soda and ½ cup vinegar and pour down the drain. Cover immediately; then rinse with hot water.

Get rid of static cling. Don't bother buying special antistatic devices—instead add ¼ cup vinegar to the washing-machine rinse cycle.

Make your own silver polish. To remove tarnish from your family silver, rub silver with a paste of baking soda and water.

Make upholstery look better and last longer with spray-on fabric guards. If a fabric guard hasn't been applied to your fabric by the manufacturer, try a fluorochemical spray (like 3-M Scotchgard), which resists water and oil-based stains.

Make baby's crib sheets out of pillowcases. They're much less expensive than special infant linens. Old pillowcases also make great garment bags. Simply cut a hole in the middle of the seam end and then slip the hanger's hook through the hole.

Use cloth diapers instead of disposables. It's about 20 percent cheaper to have a diaper service do the dirty work than it is to use disposables—and it's good for the environment.

Make your own room deodorizers. Instead of spending money on expensive sprays, simply save flowers, let their petals dry out and create your own potpourri. Then place it in bowls around the house to keep the air fragrant. You can also sew your homemade potpourri into little squares of fabric and place them in your bureau drawers to keep your family's clothes smelling sweet.

Build your own cedar closet. Instead of sending woolens and other winter clothes prone to moths out to the dry cleaner's for storage, keep them at home during the summer months. Go to a home-improvement center for some inexpensive cedar veneer (usually about 1/16-inch thick) and nail it to your own closet's walls for a home cedar cabinet.

Get plants practically free. Buy them from plant-leasing companies (see the yellow pages), which rent plants to offices. They often sell plants that can no longer be rented—for almost nothing. Large palms and ferns may cost less than $5.

Don't chop down that big oak. Large trees in the yard give off a cooling effect, potentially saving homeowners an estimated $73 a year in air-conditioning bills.

Reuse zip-lock bags. While these may cost more, they'll last longer. Zip-locks are made of heavier stuff than ordinary plastic bags and rinse out easily.

Cut or buy flowers that last a long time. The longest-lasting blooms are daisies, chrysanthemums and carnations. They'll last for a week or more, as long as you change their water each day. (These flowers are also among the least expensive varieties.)

Freeze candles. This way they'll burn more slowly and evenly.

Frame your own art. Having wall art custom-framed is usually really expensive, so go to a do-it-yourself framing shop. Store personnel will show you how to do it and will guide you in the selection of the right style and color. Also, try clip-on frames for art you're not sure you love. That way you won't drop big bucks framing a print you may be tired of in a few months.

Buy do-it-yourself machines. Ice-cream makers, sewing machines and electric saws will save bucks in the long run if you really use them.

Get furniture at cost. These days, when the furniture business is in a slump, you may be able to get into those wholesale emporiums normally open only to "the trade" (i.e., interior designers, decorators and architects). This means savings of up to 40 percent—plus you don't have to pay the middleman fees charged by decorators. On entering one of these showrooms, you may be asked if you have a "trade" card. Try responding, "No, but I have a credit card and checkbook." Chances are, you'll be in like Flynn.

Shop the streets for furnishings. Forget about department stores. Other people's castoffs could be your treasure. Some of the chicest interior designers pick tables, chairs, couches, you name it, off the sidewalks. You may need to fix these things up a bit, but sometimes you'll find antiques that an owner simply tired of. The best time for finds: Saturday mornings *early*, or the night before your garbage hauler hits the streets.

Head for secondhand furniture shops. Again, you can get great buys—and never hesitate to bargain with the proprietor. Don't always believe claims that a piece is a real Chippendale or such. (Ask for some documentation when such claims are made.) Always offer to pay in cash and chances are the seller will accept even less.

When planning to sell your home, negotiate the real estate agent's commission. Most agents ask for 6 percent of the sale price, but many are willing to take less if they really want to handle the sale of your home.

Keep your lawn well manicured. According to the National Gardening Association, good landscaping can boost a house's resale price by about 15 percent.

8
TRAVEL FOR LESS

Get a lower airfare—even after booking your ticket. When you see a lower fare advertised, call your travel agent; he/she may be able to rewrite your ticket at the cheaper rate. And when checking in for a flight, always ask if the flight's fare has dropped since you bought the ticket—if it has, you can get a refund.

Get last-minute vacation bargains. Charter services, cruise lines and hotels often give discount rates if you sign on at the last minute. While travel clubs often sell these bargains, you may have to pay a hefty membership fee to join. Instead, shop for a good travel agent who wants to help you find last-minute travel deals.

Let yourself get bumped. On domestic flights, you can get a free round-trip ticket to anywhere in the United States (or up to $400) just for waiting a few extra hours. So unless you absolutely have to get to your destination on time, volunteer to be bumped when the airline asks.

Make your own plane reservations if you don't have a fabulous travel agent. The reason? It takes lots of time for agents to uncover the best deals, and unless you give an agent lots of business, he/she may not want to be bothered finding the lowest price for you. Call airline reservationists yourself and ask them for their absolutely lowest fair. Be extremely friendly—and you may hear prices lower than those a travel agent quoted.

Special plane fares are offered for bereaved family members. If you have to fly to a funeral—or attend a loved one in an emergency—don't agree to the regular fare. Save hundreds of dollars by asking for the special "compassion rate" now offered by a number of major airlines, including Delta, American, USAir, United and Continental. Prices vary, and when such an event occurs, you won't be in any frame of mind to haggle or comparison shop, so call your travel agent and have him/her find the lowest fare. By the way, family illness or death are reasons for getting a refund for a flight—even if you bought non-refundable tickets. Sometimes a simple call to the airline customer-service desk will get you a refund. (Some airlines also require a note from a physician.)

Get plane tickets on the "gray market." This is a little risky, but if you're careful, getting tickets through "consolidators" can save you big bucks. How it works: When airlines can't sell large blocks of tickets, they dump the unsold seats at huge discounts into the hands of consolidators, who then sell them to in-the-know travel agents. There is risk involved, since some of the "gray market" companies go under without warning. But smart travel agents know how to navigate these tricky waters, so if you have one, ask for more information. Or get the book *Fly There for Less: How to Save Money Flying Worldwide* by Bob Martin (TeakWood Press, $8.95); it can be ordered by calling (800) 654-0403.

Ask for the corporate rate. Whether you're booking a hotel room, renting a car or buying a tour, always ask for the corporate rate—you'll almost always get it, no matter where you work. By the way, the corporate rate isn't always the cheapest, so you might want to ask what the lowest available rate is. Membership in certain clubs—like a frequent-flyer club—can win you a discount of up to 25 percent, but it's vital that you ask for this sort of discount; the information is rarely volunteered by reservationists.

Don't call toll-free numbers for hotel reservations. A recent survey found that those who called a hotel chain's 800 number for a room were often quoted a higher room rate. For instance, the Four Seasons in Houston charges $160 for those who dial their direct number, but the rate increases to $185 for those who use the toll-free number. Also, phone during the day because clerks on duty then are often more knowledgeable—and able to give you a good deal.

Lodge in universities. You can find safe, comfortable rooms in good locations around the world for as little as $16 a night. For more infor-

LIVING WELL OR EVEN BETTER ON LESS

mation, send $13 for "U.S. and Worldwide Travel Accommodations Guide," Campus Travel Service, Box 5007, Laguna Beach, CA 92652.

Avoid hotel phone surcharges. Hotels love to charge for the "nonservice" of allowing you to make long-distance calls from your room. But if there's no notice posted announcing a long-distance access fee, you have the right to refuse to pay it when checking out. To save money when you *are* notified of the surcharge: Push the pound (#) sign on the phone. Some hotels add $1 for each credit-card call you make; but by pushing the pound sign you can make a number of calls and be charged for only one. How it works: After the first call, let the other party hang up first; then press the pound sign without hanging up. A recording will then tell you to proceed with your next call. (But the hotel switchboard operator will think you're still on the same call!)

Ship souvenirs home duty-free. When you're abroad, you can mail gifts worth up to $50 home each day. It's a great way to cut down on potential customs duty tax when you come back with souvenirs.

Take advantage of "VAT"—value-added tax—in Europe. How it works: You get refunds on hefty sales tax (12–15 percent in many European countries, such as France and England) simply by spending a minimum amount in a store (in England, it's £50), and then getting receipts stamped by customs when you leave the country. Then mail the receipts back to the store for your refund. Get the necessary papers from the boutique and request your refund in cash, or a refund on the credit card used to make the purchase.

Go abroad to inexpensive but exotic destinations. Certain terrific places to visit, including Portugal, Spain, Greece, Turkey, Mexico, Central and South America and Puerto Rico, offer great hotels and good food at low prices—and you can find loads of inexpensive souvenirs.

Travel to places in the "shoulder season." You can pay one-third less just by waiting a week after peak season ends (travel agents call this the "shoulder season") or taking off a week before peak season begins. Talk to your travel agent to learn how and where you'll save.

Travel through a less popular airport. Often, less-trafficked airports also offer lower fares. For instance, in the New York area, it's often cheaper to fly out of Newark Airport (only 20 minutes from downtown Manhattan) than it is to take a plane from New York City's LaGuardia or Kennedy airports.

Fly midweek and save. Generally, flights are cheaper when you travel on Tuesday, Wednesday or Thursday.

Use your frequent-flyer mileage. There's been some talk in the industry that frequent-flyer programs might end in the near future, so cash in your miles while you can. Unless you're planning a big trip in the near future, cash in your miles for a better deal on a short flight. (Ask your travel agent for details.)

Join a travel club for great packages and discounts. But be careful to find a reputable club, such as Quest, Encore and Travel America. Warning: Before joining (most have a membership fee), ask for literature about the club—and never give out your credit-card number until you've thoroughly checked out the club. (Call the Better Business Bureau.)

Be an air courier. You've probably heard that travelers who act as air couriers get great deals on airfares—like $50 to London or a *free* trip to Hong Kong. Your luggage is limited to carryons (the courier service uses your checked baggage allotment for papers, contracts, etc.). Of course, there are drawbacks: You have to be ready to travel at the last minute and sometimes travel solo, and the shipper gets to decide how long you can stay at a destination before he needs you to return with more of his baggage. (Generally, you don't actually check the baggage yourself.) But if you're a free spirit, it's worth these little hassles. For more information/addresses of courier-booking services, send $14.95, including postage and handling, for the book *Insiders Guide to Air Courier Bargains;* Inwood Training Publications, Box 438T, New York, NY 10034.

Go to free attractions. These include archaeological excavation sites, battle sites (like Gettysburg National Military Park in Pennsylvania), ghost towns (like Paria Ghost Town near Kanab, Utah), museums, public gardens, wineries, breweries and distilleries (where you can often have free tastings) and more. To find these, contact state tourism departments and ask for information packets (which are also free of charge).

Travel on a Eurail Pass. Maybe you did this when you were just a teen, but there are great train deals to be had throughout Europe. Get Eurail's Flexipass, which allows five days of travel through Austria, Belgium, Denmark, Germany, Finland, France, Greece, Norway, Portugal, Spain, Sweden and other countries, within any 15-day period for just $230. This pass can only be purchased before you go abroad and can be obtained through your travel agent. For more information about other Eurail deals, write: Box 325, Old Greenwich, CT 06870. For info about BritRail (which offers train travel through the British Isles), write: 1500 Broadway, New York, NY 10036-4015; or call (212) 575-2667.

Shop for cheaper car rentals. Don't just reserve a car with the first company you call. Shop around by phone and ask about discounts. Surprisingly, corporate rates aren't always the lowest. Many rental companies offer even better rates if you have an American Express or Diners Club card, or belong to the American Automobile Association (AAA), just to name a few. When chatting with the phone reservationist, ask about these kinds of discounts—and if you qualify for more than one. It's just possible they'll add those discounts together, saving you 50 percent—or more.

Don't go for the collision-damage waiver. If your own car insurance covers rentals, or if your credit-card company provides collision insurance (American Express and Visa do, among others), you don't need it. Avoiding the CDW will really save you—it's often $10 extra for the car rental each day.

9
PET CARE
FOR LESS

Buy a low-cost pet. Hamsters and birds are all fairly inexpensive. But if you decide to spring for a dog, don't get a breed that requires tons of expensive grooming—like a poodle. Also, don't think tropical fish will be a low-maintenance or low-cost solution. They die frequently, and after you've replaced them several times, you'll realize that you could have had a dog or a cat.

Get your pet from an animal shelter. Surprisingly, some shelters specialize in purebred dogs and cats, so if you have your heart set on a pet with papers, you *don't* have to buy from an expensive breeder. What's more, these animals are always given all their shots and for a small charge are spayed or neutered. By the way, mixed-breed dogs and cats are often healthier than purebreds, which are often inbred.

Stay away from "puppy mills" or pet shop dogs and cats. These animals are often overpriced and badly bred. (Their parents are often inbred or were unhealthy animals themselves, producing potentially sickly and bad-tempered pups and kittens.)

Get pet insurance. With pet care becoming so sophisticated (and expensive), it makes sense to buy insurance. The cost ranges from $24 to $89 a year. For more information, talk to your vet or call the Animal Health Insurance Agency, Inc., (800) 345-6778.

Find an inexpensive vet. Then, take your pet for regular visits to spot problems early. And if you have more than one pet, take them to the vet at the same time and ask for a discount. Also, before bringing the pet in for minor problems, get advice from the vet over the phone. And if your pet ever needs surgery, ask if it can recover at home rather than in an expensive animal facility.

Use dry pet food instead of canned. Not only is it less costly, it's often healthier for the animal.

Give dogs rawhide bones. They last longer than plastic toys, are less messy and are healthier, too.

Bathe your dog yourself. Having your pet washed at a grooming salon is a big expense; if you don't want to wash your own dog, make it the duty of one of your kids, or hire a neighborhood teen to do it for less. Save trips to the groomer for occasional haircuts.

Toilet train your cat. Yes, really, it can be done. Saves tons on cat litter and cleanup.

Start a neighborhood pet-sitting service. Instead of paying to keep your dog or cat in a kennel whenever you're away, find friends in the neighborhood whom you trust to come around during the day to feed/walk your pet. You can swap favors with other pet-owning neighbors by offering to take care of their pets while they're away.

10
SHOPPING FOR LESS

Make a list before you head for the supermarket. You'll be less likely to cruise the aisles and fill your cart with items you don't really need. By the way, in most supermarkets, staples (milk, bread, fruit, vegetables and meat) are located along the perimeter of the store; prepared foods are usually found in the inner aisles. To keep yourself and your kids from picking up this expensive (and often fattening) stuff, stick to the outer edges of the store.

Clip coupons. The latest study shows Americans save more than $3 billion a year by redeeming supermarket and manufacturers' coupons. But don't use them unless they're for the brands you usually buy. Otherwise, you'll end up spending more than you would ordinarily. Keep coupons on the refrigerator door (under a magnet) and check them against your shopping list before you go to the store.

Always get a rain check. When you take the time to go to a store's sale and the advertised special has already disappeared, be sure to get a rain check for that item when it's next in stock; many states have rain-check rules, requiring that stores offer the same price when they get the item back in stock. Don't be persuaded into buying a similar product for more money.

Wise up to "sale" jargon. For instance, an item marked "on sale" was once priced higher and may return to that price. "Clearance sale" means the item has probably been reduced substantially in price. "Promotional sale" may refer to an item not usually sold at that store—and chances are the savings will be small. What's a really good sale? One where the price has been marked down by at least 40 percent.

Check warranties religiously. The length of the guarantee offered should figure into which item you purchase. For instance, if two TV sets offer similar features and prices, take the one that offers the best warranty. Also, remember that some of the large credit-card companies offer free extended warranties for items purchased with their cards.

Buy generic brands whenever possible. You know generics are great savers at the supermarket (best for sugar, milk, flour and orange juice), but you can also get generic pharmaceuticals (like aspirin and antihistamines) and even prescription drugs. A brand-name drug can cost 50 percent more than the generic version, and they have the exact same ingredients. (For more information, get a free copy of "Smart Consumer's Guide to Prescription Drugs" by writing to: Guide to Prescription Drugs, AARP Fulfillment, 1909 K Street, N.W., Washington, DC 20049.)

Avoid buying bum products. Send for "Quackery," a guide to help consumers tell if a product sounds too good to be true. Write to: Consumer Information Center, Department 528V, Pueblo, CO 81009. Free.

Stock up *after* Christmas. Gift wrap, Christmas cards, decorations, tree ornaments and other items are sure to be marked half-price or less after the holidays. Likewise, get half-price Valentine's Day chocolates and Easter goodies after those holidays, too.

Shop when the weather's frightful. The reason? There's less competition in the form of fellow customers for the fabulous stuff on sale. By the way, the biggest sale months are January and August, when prices are slashed to get rid of old inventory and make room for the new.

Negotiate prices for electronic/stereo equipment. How to do it? First, offer to pay in full, in cash. Even nice retail establishments are open to charging less if they don't have to deal with credit cards and layaways. If delivery is offered free of charge, ask if you can take it home yourself—and pay a few dollars less. Also, stores are often anxious to get rid of certain "stray" components. Let them make you a package deal. Pay the full price for that stereo receiver, but ask to pay at least 25 percent less on the cassette deck and CD player—in these hard times, they'll probably say okay. At the very least, get the store to throw in something like a cartridge for a turntable or some blank audio- or videocassettes (the markup on these items is tremendous).

Master the art of haggling. Be gentle when you negotiate. Ask if the store is planning to put the item on sale. If the clerk says, "Maybe in a month or two," say you'll take it right now for "x" amount (about 20 percent) less. The worst he'll say is no. The stores with the most flexible policies tend to be those mom-and-pop, family-owned establishments. The reason: The owner, who may be helping you, knows how much—or how little—he/she can charge you and still make a profit. Plus, since he/she's the boss, no prices need to be cleared with a supervisor. The toughest places to get a discount: big chain stores, where prices are listed in a computerized inventory. Still, it's possible to get a discount at these places, especially on slightly damaged items, by talking to the clerks at the customer-service desk.

Save deposit cans and bottles and redeem them. It's good for the environment, and those nickels do add up. Make collecting and separating them a chore for your kids—then let them keep the proceeds, instead of paying allowances.

Go for factory seconds or "imperfects." Many companies offer deep discounts for slightly imperfect merchandise—and usually it's impossible to spot the imperfection. Best bets for clothing: seconds in underwear, panty hose and shoes. For instance, 12 pairs of L'eggs factory seconds cost less than half the regular price. Also, you can often get good buys on seconds in sheets, blankets, towels, dishes and other housewares. Find them at factory outlets (see Chapter 5: Dressing for Less) or at such "name-brands-for-less" stores as Marshalls and T. J. Maxx.

Order housewares, clothes, gardening equipment and more from catalogs. They're often less expensive than what you'll find in department stores.

Don't chuck your dinnerware pattern because a few dishes have been broken. Even if your pattern has been discontinued, it's possible to find replacements through china search services. Here are two: Patterns Unlimited, P.O. Box 15238, Seattle, WA 98115; and Topex, 58 Linda Lane, Tiffin, OH 44883. (Send a self-addressed, stamped envelope to Tiffin.) How it works: Write to these sources, giving your pattern name, the pieces you're looking for and the number you need. If you don't know the name of the pattern, send a photo of the front of a plate, along with another shot of the markings on the back. These sources will let you know if your pattern is in stock; if it isn't, they'll search for it, free of charge. When they find it, you're charged the retail price of the item, plus shipping.

11
GIVING
FOR LESS

Buy fun gift items on sale. Even when it isn't Christmas or somebody's birthday, it's smart to buy undesignated presents. The reason: You'll save on stocking stuffers at Christmastime (when they're selling at top price), and you'll have a great gift on hand for those times when someone presents you with a gift—and you didn't think to buy one for them. (You'll have an inexpensive gift or two at the ready in the closet.)

Make your own fancy vinegar bottles. Get a pretty bottle and fill it with vinegar, adding a pretty, flavorful herb like basil or a small fruit like raspberries.

Give homemade houseplants. Take cuttings from your most exotic plants, grow them in a glass of water and then plant them in a pretty pot.

Give your own best baked goods. Bake your renowned scratch pies, cakes or cookies and package them in a pretty tin. (You can also dress them up in tissue paper.) Homemade goodies make a great, inexpensive gift (especially at Christmas) for coworkers and neighbors.

Offer your personal services as a gift. Make up a coupon saying you will baby-sit, cook a meal, type a paper, drive the car pool, give a manicure—to a friend or family member.

Get a better deal on bouquets. Instead of calling long-distance flower services, which generally charge more and offer rather dull arrangements, call a florist's shop in the city/town where your recipient lives. How to find a good shop? Call the local hospital and ask the desk nurse which florists send the prettiest—and least costly—bouquets. She/he is sure to know.

Make your own dried-flower arrangements. It's not hard to do. Take cut flowers, and before they've finished blooming, take them out of water, tie them together and hang them upside down for a couple of weeks. Do this with a number of different flowers and/or greens and then place them in a pretty bowl or basket for a great, sweet-smelling gift that costs practically nothing.

Make up gift baskets. There are all sorts of expensive boutiques cropping up that pile gifts in a basket—and then charge an arm and a leg for it. Instead, do it yourself for much less. Buy some plain straw baskets in interesting shapes. Hand-paint them (or have your kids do it); you can cover them completely in color or paint on designs. Then, fill them with inexpensive toiletries, such as soap, a hand-massage glove, some bath oil, or with your own dried-flower arrangement for a pretty and inexpensive birthday gift for a friend or relative. The cost could be as low as $10—much less than you'd spend on clothing or jewelry.

Give away gifts you've gotten—but never used. It's not a tacky practice at all. Everyone gets gifts they simply can't use—and have no way of returning. If you have a really good idea that someone else would love that dress/vase/necklace or whatever, wrap it beautifully and give it to them. It's smarter than letting the unwanted (but nice) object gather dust in your closet.

Bring back unique items when you travel. You know that certain objects that are expensive here can be bought in foreign countries for far less. For instance, silver jewelry can be had for a few dollars in Mexico. So when vacationing, be sure to bring back a lot of these inexpensive treasures—even if you don't know who to give them to. They're sure to come in handy for a birthday or Christmas gift. And because the present (perhaps a beautiful handicraft) was purchased abroad, it will seem more valuable and cherishable to the giftee.